Good

How to be Good in a Bad World

By Ringo Calhoun

Timely Publishing

Why You Need to Read this Book

Are you frustrated with the way the world seems to be crumbling around us? Do you feel terrible when you watch the news and see bad people doing bad things? Does rudeness and lack of consideration for other people seem to be the norm these days? Do you wish people could be better and nicer?

If you answered yes to these questions, you are ready to make an important choice and then act on it: be a good person. It may seem at times like one person can't make a difference, but when each one of us makes the choice to be better and to do good things, we can change the world. Start with you.

In this book you will learn about what it means to be good, what good people do and how they behave in ordinary and extraordinary situations, the most destructive of bad characteristics to avoid, how not to lose heart when you see all the badness around you, and concrete actions you can take to be a better person.

When you decide to take that step and be a good person in a bad world, you will be inspiring others to do the same and you will amplify the good that you do. You will also make your own life better. Being good and being kind to others will improve both your physical and mental health and will lead to greater satisfaction with your life. By being good you help yourself, you help other people, and you help the world to be a better place.

Table of Contents

Introduction – Being Good: What's in it for You?

You may think that being good is all about what you can do for others. It's true that this is a large part of what it means to be good. Sure, you can be good to yourself, but being good really happens when you care for and treat others well. It's a complicated topic and there are many aspects to the definition of being good and also many consequences.

Maybe you think you have always been good. Maybe you are of the opinion that people, yourself included, are basically good. You generally do good, treat people well, make responsible decisions, and take care of yourself and those you love. You might think that there isn't much more to it than that.

On the other hand, maybe you have been worried that you don't always make the best, or the most ethical decisions; the decisions that you think will make the world a better place. Whatever has led you to read up on this subject, there is one important question that is probably at the back of your mind: why should I be try any harder to be good?

Being good isn't just about helping others. Making the world a better place and making life easier or better for other people are wonderful reasons for doing more good, but it's also OK to think about you. How will being a good person affect you? How will you benefit from being and behaving like a better person? In other words, why should you bother with all of this? Here are several reasons to consider taking this journey toward becoming and even better person:

Being Good Spreads the Good
Research has shown that the people you surround yourself with impacts how you feel, act, and behave towards others. This means that if you spend time with happy people, you are more likely to be happy too. Emotions, both positive and negative, spread like a virus through social circles, but so do behaviors. If you behave like a good person, others will do the same. Your goodness can be spread like a contagious disease making life around you better and more pleasant the more good you do.

Being Good Improves Your Relationships
Following on the previous point, if you are being good and doing kind things, your spouse or partner will be positively influenced. As both of you begin to live better and kinder lives you will be better to each other. You will automatically be happier with each other, happier in general, and less argumentative.

Compassion is Good for Your Health

Being compassionate is an important part of being a good person. It means trying to understand the pain of others and empathizing with people. Beyond the empathy, it also means doing something to help make the situation better. For instance, if you have a friend who is feeling anxious that she might lose her job, recognize and acknowledge how she is feeling. Try to help her feel better about her situation. That is being compassionate, whereas someone who is not compassionate would simply ignore her feelings and write them off as not significant.

Research has demonstrated that people who are compassionate and loving towards others are generally happier, feel less depressed, and are more satisfied with life. Compassionate people are even in better physical condition and are fitter than those who are not very compassionate. Research has also shown that people who are compassionate have stronger immune systems and resist illness better.

Kind People Understand Others Better

When you are compassionate, loving, and kind toward other people, you are better able to understand them. Studies have proven that being compassionate and kind increases a person's ability to understand what someone else is going through, or in other words to be empathetic. If you act kindly you will be better able to communicate with people because you will be able to interpret what they are thinking and feeling more accurately.

Kindness Makes You Less Afraid

Fear is an emotion that holds people back. When you are afraid, you don't take action and you don't take risks that could end up paying off in the long run. Fear also prevents us from helping others, even when we know it's the right thing to do. Your life will be immeasurably better if you are less afraid. The good news is that being kind, compassionate, and empathetic reduces fear. Studies have proven that when people were given training in being compassionate, they were less afraid to help others and less afraid in general.

Gratitude Makes You Happy

Being grateful for what you have and for what others do for you is an important part of being good. No one likes someone who is ungrateful. A lot of recent research has pinpointed gratitude as a major factor in overall happiness and satisfaction with life.

In one study a group of participants were asked to write down what they were grateful for every day while another group wrote down complaints and a control group wrote about anything. After ten weeks the people in the group that expressed gratitude were feeling better about their lives. They were more optimistic, felt happier, exercised more often, and visited the doctor less frequently than the people who complained for ten weeks or those who were free to write about anything.

Another study demonstrated that just one act of gratitude could make you feel better immediately. Participants were asked to write a letter to thank and show gratitude to someone they felt had never really been thanked for a kindness. Right after doing this the participants showed a huge increase in their scores on a happiness measurement scale.

Being Ethical at Work Pays
Being good also has an economic benefit. In a study about business ethics, a group of participants was shown two products and were told that one was produced using ethical standards and the other was not. The ethical standards under consideration included fair treatment of employees, environmentally sustainable processes, and respect for human rights in manufacturing.

The results demonstrated that people are overwhelmingly willing to pay at least a little bit more for products that were manufactured and sold according to ethical standards. They were even more willing to punish those companies who were known to not adhere to ethics. In business, it's clear: being good pays.

There are so many reasons to be good, but don't make the mistake of thinking that your own well-being isn't one of them. In order to do good for others, you have to be self-aware, satisfied, happy, compassionate, and kind. In other words you have to look out for yourself too. You can't embody all of these wonderful traits if you are not caring for your own needs. Being good should be about you and about others.

Ethics: What Does it all Mean?

When people talk about being good, two different words tend to come up most often: ethics and morality. Sometimes you hear variations of these terms like, ethical or unethical, moral or immoral, or morals or ethic. To understand what it is to be a good person, it's important to understand what these terms mean and what the differences are. Here are a couple of standard definitions from Merriam-Webster.com:

Ethics –

1. the discipline dealing with what is good and bad and with moral duty and obligation
2. a set of moral principles; a theory or system of moral values; the principles of conduct guiding an individual or group; a guiding philosophy

Morality –

1. beliefs about what is right behavior and what is wrong behavior
2. the degree to which something is right and good

Dictionary definitions sometimes need clarification. Here are a few important points to take from these definitions:

Discipline vs. beliefs
Ethics is a discipline. In other words it is a field of study, often included as a part of philosophy. Academic thinkers consider whether behaviors and actions are right or wrong when they discuss ethics. They also investigate how to determine if something is right or wrong and what that means to different people and cultures.

Morality's definition, on the other hand, includes the word belief. Morals are more strongly connected to an individual's beliefs of what is right or wrong than to any kind of academic discourse and consensus.

Guiding principles
The definition of ethics includes describing them as a set of principles, a theory, or a set of moral values that guide one person or a group of people. This implies that ethics are constructed to be used to determine behaviors. Thought goes into creating ethical guidelines.

Morality is more abstract in this respect. Morality is not necessarily a well-thought out set of guiding principles. It is more an inherent belief in what feels right and what feels wrong.

Ethics need morality

While there are some important differences between these two terms, note that the definitions of ethics include morality or morals. You cannot create a set of ethical guidelines to dictate your behavior without considering what is moral, or what is right or wrong.

Because the following chapters are designed to guide you through the process of actively becoming a good person, we will largely use the term ethics to describe what we are doing. Everyone has morality or a sense of morals without needing to think about it too much. Ethics, however, are planned and carefully considered. To consciously decide to be a good person means you will be embarking on the creation of an ethical framework in which to live your life and with which to guide your actions. It will be underlain with your morals, but you are crafting ethics here.

Ethics: What Do the Experts Say?

As you work to create ethical guidelines for your life it is important to consider what others have had to say on the topic of ethical behavior and being good. You should craft your own framework and principles, but there is no need to totally reinvent the wheel. Philosophers have been discussing ethics for millennia. Don't make the mistake of thinking you don't need to know what they discovered. A complete treatise on the history and philosophy of ethics would take up several volumes, but here's a quick rundown:

Plato

Considered to be the father of all Western thinking, Plato was a philosopher who lived in ancient Greece during the fourth century B.C. His description of ethics can be boiled down to a fairly simple description of right and wrong. He said that knowledge is good and ignorance is bad. If you know what is good and right, in other words, you can do good and be ethical. He believed that knowledge and goodness began with self-awareness. If you are self-aware, you will know what is good and what is not. Study, debate, and thinking are required to decide what is good and right and what is bad and wrong.

Consequentialism

The idea of consequentialism is that you can determine whether an action or behavior is good, moral or ethical by considering the outcome of the action. An action that is good is one that produces a good outcome. Of course, this raises many questions: What is a good outcome? For whom should the outcome be good? Who gets to judge the goodness of an outcome?

There are many subcategories of consequentialism, such as utilitarianism as outlined by famous ethicist John Stuart Mill. According to utilitarianism, an action is good if it causes the most happiness for the greatest number of people. It's a pretty practical and straightforward guiding principal, but sometimes it means that certain people fall on the wrong side of an ethical decision, while others benefit.

Negative consequentialism focuses on minimizing negative outcomes instead of promoting positive outcomes. Egoism focuses on producing outcomes that are good for the self, while asceticism states that the self is less important and that outcomes should be maximized for others, not oneself.

Deontology

Deontology is a family of ethical philosophies that focuses on the rightness or wrongness of the actual actions and behaviors, rather than on the consequences. Deontologists focus on their duties and the rights of others when making ethical decisions. People who use religion to dictate behavior follow a form of deontology. They consider certain guidelines to be good because they came from God, not because of positive outcomes.

Philosopher Immanuel Kant espoused a form of deontology called the categorical imperative. He believed that right behavior should be dictated by duty. He also believed that what made a behavior or action good was the motive of the person engaging in that action, regardless of the consequences. In other words, if your intentions are good, you are doing something good, no matter what happens as the result of your actions.

The Natural Rights Theory, which came from such famous ethicists and thinkers and Thomas Hobbes and John Locke, holds that all humans have certain rights that are natural and absolute and that being ethical means making sure that all people have these rights. This was the foundation of today's idea of human rights and the U.S. Bill of Rights.

Virtue Ethics

According to virtue ethics, actions and their consequences are less important to ethics than the nature of a person. If a person is virtuous and behavers virtuously, then he or she will be good. The idea of virtue ethics goes all the way back to ancient Greece, but has become popular again in modern times. Feminist thinkers and writers, for instance, have emphasized the traditional virtues of women as a model for right behavior: care for others, nurturing, patience, and self-sacrifice.

Meta-Ethics

Meta-ethics is a branch of ethical philosophy that is concerned with debating the meaning of ethical statements. It tries to understand ethical judgements, statements, and attitudes and defends or denies them. It is a truly academic field and one that is interesting, yet doesn't always add anything practical to the discussion of what is right or wrong.

Applied Ethics

Applied ethics is where ethical philosophy gets really practical. It refers to the application of ethical ideas and philosophies to the creation of usable guidelines. For instance, physicians and other health care professionals work according to medical ethics. They have a set of guidelines to follow, which have been set out to ensure that patients are well cared for and treated with respect and dignity.

Applied ethics have also been used to set guidelines for the practice of law, for psychological experiments, for all types of scientific research, for business, for how we interact with the natural environment, and for the way the media works, just to name a few.

Is Human Nature Good, Bad, or Neutral?

It is an eternal question: Are we essentially good? Ask different people and you will get many different answers. Philosophers have been debating and thinking on this for thousands of years. Is there a definitive answer? Probably not, but perspective makes a big difference.

If you have had a pretty good life, if you have been generally treated well by people and never experienced abuse or bullying, you would probably say that people are generally good. A lot of us would say that, even if we have experienced some mean or bad people. Many of us can probably say that the majority of people we encounter every day are nice and mostly good. But are these ordinary people good because they are trying to be good or because it comes naturally to them?

Consider another perspective: You watch the world news every night, and it's grim. You see people being killed in wars, innocent bystanders being caught in terrorist acts, criminals torturing and killing people, stealing from people, and generally hurting others. You see that human activity continues to degrade the environment and put wildlife at risk.

You don't even have to watch the news to get this perspective. If you watch many reality television programs you see people behaving selfishly and terribly toward others. They cut each other down just to try to get to the prize at the end of the competition. How can you see all of this badness and not assume we are inherently bad, or at least neutral, and that we require concerted effort to be good?

Maybe you should look at answering the question of whether or not humans are good by nature by looking at yourself. Do you feel bad when you do something bad? Does it feel better to do something good? When you do something bad, or hurt someone else, do you then naturally feel compelled to make up for it in some way? When we look internally, it seems like we are basically good. To do bad things and to hurt other people, animals, and the natural environment feels wrong for most of us.

To get an answer to the question you can turn to philosophers or religion. Philosophers have already given this some serious thought. Plato and his student Aristotle both came to the conclusion that humans are rational and social, but does that make us good? They also said that we can be easily corrupted by things like power.

Ethicist and philosopher, and proponent of the Natural Rights Theory, Thomas Hobbes, famously said that humans in their natural state live lives that are "solitary, poor, nasty, brutish, and short." He clearly thought we were not naturally good and that we needed to outline and enforce things like human rights and ethical principles.

Jean-Jacques Rousseau, living in pre-revolutionary France claimed that human nature wasn't fixed. He agreed with Hobbes that we were once pretty nasty creatures, but as time went on we became more enlightened. Rousseau believed in human potential and thought that human nature could become good with time, and with science, learning, and culture. He also claimed that we are all basically driven by selfishness. In the modern world, this isn't hard to believe.

Philosophers are not the only ones to have weighed in on the essence of human nature with respect to good and evil. As science developed in the 1800s, people like Sigmund Freud and Charles Darwin used psychology and biology to try to answer the question. Freud saw us as being in a constant struggle between our biological urges, our selfishness, and our higher selves, the part of us interested in doing good. Darwin didn't have much to say directly about human nature, but his Theory of Evolution forced a major shift in how we think about ourselves as animals first and humans second.

Religion and religious philosophers have ideas about human nature too. Much of western religion points to humans as being bad and needing God to point the way to goodness. St. Augustine wrote about original sin and said that we are born bad, selfish, and broken. Only through God can we be good. Many eastern religions on the other hand suggest that we are generally good, but can be molded by our experiences to be good or evil.

Today, research scientists are making serious attempts to answer the big question about human nature. For instance, one large study investigated whether the natural human instinct is to be selfish or to work together; the former would imply we are naturally bad and the latter is assumed to show we are inherently good. The researchers really wanted to look at intuition, that is, an automatic reaction, to answer the question. They wanted to avoid reflection, which is when we have time to think about and consider our actions. Do people intuitively and instinctually cooperate or behave selfishly first?

Using over 800 participants the researchers asked people to make quick, intuitive decisions about money. The participants could either make a choice that would maximize their own financial gains, or a choice that would maximize the gains for the group as a whole. What the researchers found was heartening. People overwhelmingly chose to help the group first when they had to make a decision quickly. When given time to reflect, they were more likely to make a selfish choice. The implication is that we are intuitively cooperative and not selfish. It suggests that our nature is to be good to each other.

Similar studies followed this one with over 2,000 participants and using a variety of different types of activities and choices that were clearly divided between being selfish and being cooperative. The results were always the same: we naturally tend to help the group, not ourselves as individuals.

Another study used babies to try to determine what our basic human nature is. Babies can enlighten us because they are relatively uninfluenced by the world around them. They have yet to experience much of human nature or to have been influenced by cultural factors. They can't read or speak, and they don't have friends to motivate their behaviors. Babies, in other words, are innocent. If they naturally tend towards good, then it says a lot about human nature.

In one study, which must have been adorable, babies were shown a simple puppet show in which one puppet struggled and two others either helped or hindered it. The babies were allowed to reach for whichever puppet they preferred, and overwhelmingly chose the helper puppet. They also demonstrated surprise, as measured by staring, when the puppet needing help showed a preference for the not-so-nice, hindering puppet.

Neither of these studies is conclusive, nor do they give us a definite answer to our question. We may never have an answer to the question of whether or not we are inherently good, bad, or neutral. However, the modern studies are powerful. They clearly demonstrate that we tend towards good. Our natural instincts are to help others, not to be selfish, and we are naturally drawn to those who are good.

While we can't fully prove it, knowing that human nature is essentially good is a big boost. You don't have to work against inherently selfish, nasty tendencies. You already have a leg up on being good. Now you just need to learn how to get past some of the meaner and more selfish tendencies you do have and how to live a life as an upright, good, and compassionate person.

<u>Character, Values, and Morals</u>

When you think of what it means to be a good person, do you have someone in mind? Or do you have to use your imagination to conjure up someone who is truly good? Whether you can point to someone you know, someone in the public eye, or someone you have created in your imagination, it isn't hard recognize good when you see it. It also isn't difficult to recognize a person who is good when we encounter him or her.

You would probably say that this good person has character. She has a great character and that is part of what makes her a good person. You also might describe someone as having good values or values similar to your own, or values that you hope to emulate and take on as your own. A good person is also often described as being moral. You can recognize a good person with good intentions and good actions, but what does it all mean?

Let's start with character. We all have character. Your character is what makes you unique and an individual. Character refers to the qualities, typically moral, ethical and mental, that make a person unique and different from every other individual. From this perspective, to say that someone is good because they have character doesn't hold water. Character can be good and it can be bad. It is your personality, your temperament, your mental makeup and it is complicated. It's who you are at your core, even when no one else is watching.

There is another way in which we use the term character, though. You might say that your friend Sally is a real character. What you probably mean when you say that is that Sally has a strong personality. She makes people laugh or she behaves in ways that are quirky or unconventional. She's a character, like she was written for a movie or a novel.

We also use the term character to describe something admirable in a person. Gary really has character; he's a great guy. This is when we use the term to indicate goodness in someone, but what does it mean?

It means that the traits that make up his personality and who he is as a person, down deep, are admirable and good. It means that he has certain personality traits that guide him to do the right thing in most situations. His character is good, so he does good things. Stating that someone has character also implies that he is not flat or personality-less. He stands for something and he is firm in his beliefs, even when there is no personal benefit.

If you want to be a good person, you want people to say about you that you have character. You want your character, whatever makes it up, to be clear to those around you. You want people to know that, for instance, part of your character is to be kind to others, and that you are always kind to people, to the best of your ability and to the extent any given situation allows. Good people have strong and sturdy characters. When you're around them you know what their character is, who they are, and how that will guide their actions. You can count on them because they have strong ethical standards and integrity.

What about values then? What are they and how do they make you a good or a bad person? Values are a set of standards, principles, ideas, and things or people that you deem important to your life or life in general. You use them to guide your actions throughout your life and they can be good or bad.

Most people tend to get their values from their parents or whoever raised them. Parents talk about instilling their values in their children. As you grow into an adult you can decide to change your values based on your experiences and your own ideas of what is important and how you should behave. Doing so is not always easy. What we learn as children can be difficult to change.

Sometimes we describe people as being good because they have good values. What this typically means is that those values match ours, not that they meet some objective standard for goodness. For example, one of your important values might be spending time with family. When you meet other people who also value spending time with family, you might say that they are good or have good values. What if you met someone who doesn't value family time because her family isn't very nice? Just because her values don't match yours does not mean she isn't a good person.

Values are subjective and to say that someone is good because he has values is misleading. What if someone values materialistic things? Does that make him good? It doesn't, but what it does that is useful is it tells you a lot about his character and what you can expect from him.

Unlike character, which is more innate, values are something you can plan out and change. If you were raised to value the right to own a gun, but you have become sickened by gun violence, you can change that value. You can decide that peace and safety are more valuable than the right to bear arms. To be a good person you definitely need to have values, but carefully consider what those are and what about your current values you may need to change to be a better person. These values drive your behaviors, so think on them carefully.

Finally, we have the statement that a good person is a moral person. Is this necessarily true? And what does it mean to be moral? We defined morality earlier and contrasted it with ethics. For most of this book we want to stick with being ethical. The reason is that morality is often skewed and misunderstood. It's also highly relative. What one person, religion, or culture considers moral could be immoral to another.

Being moral means following guidelines for behavior, but there are many different such guidelines. Should you follow the morality set out by Christianity or Judaism? Or should you consider the morality of Eastern religions and philosophies? Morality is closely tied to religion and that can be problematic when deciding how to be good.

Following the morals of a particular religion can be good, but it can also go awry. For instance, many would say that the Christian faith believes that homosexuality is immoral. You have gay friends or family and you love them. You think they are good people, but according to Christian moral guidelines there is something inherently immoral about them. It just doesn't mesh with your experience or your sense of what is right and wrong.

In deciding how to be a good person character and values are essential to consider. Morality as defined by any one group, culture, or religion is less important. Trying to follow any one pre-defined moral code strictly is bound to cause you problems. You could say that you will create your own morality, which is fine, but it is much the same as developing and outlining your values. You can also decide to follow the basic morality of, say Christianity. To you that may mean following the example of Jesus and being kind, compassionate, and loving. You are using the essential message of Christianity to be your moral compass while eschewing other so-called morals that don't jive with your world view and your sense of goodness.

As you go through this journey of becoming a good, or better, person, think about your character and your values. Ask friends and family how they would describe your character. You might be surprised. How others view your character says a lot about who you are. Also spend time considering and firmly deciding what you value. Your values will be a huge part of what guides you to be good.

<u>Characteristics of Good People</u>

As you figure out how to be good, it can be helpful to make some careful and detailed definitions of what makes a person good. You have already thought about your own character. Are you satisfied with it? Do you want to change and to develop characteristics that are more in line with being good? If so, you need to know what characteristics define goodness.

Honor

When it comes down to it, honor sounds like an extremely outdated word. Surely it's meant to be applied to knights from the Middle Ages who went around saving damsels from dragons, or medieval peasants dying to protect their patch of turnip field. These aren't exactly important parts of modern life. But honor is more than just the application of an outdated notion of noble civility; honor has to do with sticking to your guns, and remaining true to those who've earned your trust.

Although it might seem to be a pretty vague difference, honor and honesty/loyalty are distinctly separate beasts. Honesty and loyalty are internal characteristics, while honor has more to do with how you treat other people. Honor is something you earn through the eyes of the people around you, and how they interpret your actions and your words as being decent and fair.

Being honorable isn't the same as being liked by everyone. In fact, being honorable can sometimes involve standing by the unpopular opinion because it's the one you know to be true. Making the right decision based on ethical reasons, as opposed to selfish or personal reasons, is a key part of being honorable. Basically, having integrity, which we'll cover later, is an important part of becoming an honorable person, and the faith in your convictions to stand by what you believe is correct in a non-confrontational, but firm, way.

Understanding the concept of honor is vital if you want to become an honorable person. As this is based mostly on how other people interpret your actions, this isn't something you can wake up in the morning and just resolve to do; this is a long-term application of your desire to be a better human being, one that will prove invaluable in the long run.

Becoming honorable takes the time and effort to become a consistently trustworthy, integral person. An important part of this is honesty. Honesty does not mean blurting your opinion when it is not wanted or needed, or putting forth your opinion on a subject as being greater or more important than someone else's.

Honesty means the ability to convey your thoughts succinctly and politely, but with enough certainty that they were worth adding to the conversation. It is not your job to force your idea down someone else's throat; it is your job to present that idea in a way that gives respect to everyone else contributing to the conversation.

Important too in becoming honorable is standing by what you believe to be right. This can be in terms of an idea, as above, or indeed a person. For example, if everyone else has decided that Jerry from your friend group isn't really welcome any more for no apparent reason, make sure you're the one to question it.

You don't need to shout them down; just ask the person who you believe is doing something unfair to justify their actions. If they can, don't be afraid to change your mind, but be sure that you've established that you won't allow people to be bullied or ostracized for no reason, even if it risks your own social status.

Another important aspect of being honorable is being a good listener. Listening means you can gather information to make an informed decision on matters and take your time to weigh the options and evidence, so when you do talk you'll have a strong idea of what it is you want to say. Speaking your mind isn't an issue, but be sure that you know your mind before you speak up.

So why should you be honorable? Being honorable is often considered rather an old-fashioned way of thinking, but it has many real-world applications today. Employers will look for people who know their own mind and can speak eloquently and without going round and round in circles about their ideas. The ability to be confident in your opinions and decisions is an attractive one, as it signals somebody who doesn't make snap judgments that they later regret. With so much um-ing and ah-ing in the professional field, the ability to stick to your guns is a highly valued one.

Having a strong ethical or value code that you stick to at all times, whether the situation is social, professional, or otherwise, is an extremely attractive quality in friends, co-workers, and potential partners alike. You don't need to go out there throwing how ethically sound you are in people faces, but set out boundaries within yourself that you consistently follow.

The strength of will and self-assurance to do the right thing will likely land you with a group of friends who do the same thing and are also trustworthy, as you'll find yourself questioning those who aren't. On a side note, make sure no one you know is deliberately acting the victim or feeding you false information because they know that you'll feel you have to react in some way. Working out the false flags from people in need of some kind of help takes time, but you'll get there.

Honor will help you feel more comfortable with your decisions. If you sit down and work out a specific moral code for yourself—the things that you will and won't put up with, situations where you will or won't intervene—you can be sure that the choices you make are not based on outside pressure or the influence of others, but rather on the set of ethics that you have defined for yourself and that you are comfortable with. It's a long road that takes a while to secure completely, but becoming an honorable person will benefit both you, and everyone around you, in the long run.

Honesty

Miguel de Cervantes is often quoted as saying "honesty is the best policy". But what precisely did he mean by honesty? The word has come to mean a wide variety of different things (how many times have you heard "I'm just being honest" used to justify a grievous insult to the listener?), but establishing precisely what it means in relation to being a good person is vital.

Honesty is, simply, making the decision to tell the truth whenever you can. Notice that this doesn't say "always," as telling the truth can sometimes be a huge, unnecessary blow to someone's feelings. There are times when directly expressing the thoughts in your head likely won't end with rapturous applause.

That said, there are occasions where the truth will hurt someone's feelings, but it must be told anyway. A big part of honesty is recognizing the occasions during which you have a duty to be honest. These can be tricky to pin down, but establishing when the truth needs to be told, and how to tell it, will move you beyond those who use "honesty" as an excuse for outright meanness or cruelty.

Sometimes being honest requires you to be completely blunt and straightforward, such as telling someone that their business idea simply won't get off the ground, or dissuading someone from buying a too-small outfit. Other times you should be a little gentler.

How do you tell the difference? Generally, you can be more honest later if the decision you're being honest about hasn't yet been made, as all you are doing is attempting to help your friend avoid disaster. A degree of tact should be used when it comes to decisions that have already been made, as it's likely they will want some form of reassurance, as opposed to the cold, hard truth of their failure. Use your tact, and try not to offend anyone.

Sure, there are plenty of opportunities for you to be verbally honest in your day-to-day life—you're just working out how to tell people that cutting their hair short or quitting their job to open a cat sweater store probably isn't the best idea they've ever had—but there are many non-verbal applications of honesty in real life too.

For example, actually carrying out tasks that you've agreed to do is a powerful sign of honesty. If you can't do something, the ability to say "look, I just won't have the time to do this to a high enough standard" is admirable, but the ability to prioritize the work you've promised for other people and make sure it gets done is a strong message to send. Similarly, the ability to stand up and acknowledge your mistakes, to disallow anyone else to take the blame, and to establish why and how you made the mistake in the first place, will help restore the trust in you people may have lost when you made the mistake in the first place.

A big part of being honest is being true to yourself. It's all well and good to share your opinion in a reasonable manner when it's required, but covering up some facet of who you are to make someone else happy isn't honest. This doesn't mean you have to run around shops and supermarkets declaring everything you ever did in the sixth grade; it means being open and truthful about your experiences and actions in the past, and putting the truth of the situation before any potential repercussions for yourself. Being upfront about who you are is important in becoming a good person in general, as it will allow you to build yourself up from a place of honesty.

Being honest all the time will, for a start, help you to earn the trust of your friends, family and co-workers. Making sure not to gossip or spread rumors that have been told to you in confidence will establish your reputation as one to discuss these matters with (which can, granted, be somewhat of a double-edged sword depending on who your friends, family and co-workers are).

It also means that people will trust your opinion to be true, and will more often come to you for advice about important matters that need your input. While you won't be able to give scintillating advice to each and every one of them, chances are that your honesty will help nudge them in the right direction to make their final decision. This is mostly useful in the work arena, where many people mollycoddle or defer to the opinions of their higher ups; the ability to state, with confidence, what you think is infinitely useful here.

In the same way, honesty will allow you to establish deeper bonds with your friends. If people feel they can come to you without fear of judgment and be given a properly truthful answer on the topic at hand, you'll soon find yourself helping a lot of friends, and, as they'll likely feel comfortable in returning your honesty, you'll also find yourself with a lot of friends to return the favor and help you when you need it.

Making a choice not to lie about who you are, which so many of us do on a daily basis to avoid confrontation or embarrassment, will allow you to seek out friends and romantic partners who have had the same experiences as you, but perhaps had not before found anyone to share it with. Surrounding yourself with people who know the real you—and even still kind of like it—will encourage you to be more comfortable and more truthful about who you are as a person.

Integrity

As George Eadie so memorably said, "If you don't stand for something, you will fall for anything". This is an important quote to remember as you start your journey towards becoming a person with more integrity.

Integrity is the hardcore belief that your convictions and choices are one of the most important things about you, and sticking to those choices is even more important. You'll often hear the words "character" and "integrity" used as part of one package. That's because so many people see integrity as a vital part of what defines us a human beings. The strength of conviction to stand beside what we've done, and acknowledge whether or not it was the right thing to do, is simply the key in successfully establishing your personality and your ethical code.

Integrity has many definitions, but they all essentially boil down to the same concept: if you have integrity, you will always do what you believe is right, no matter what the circumstances. Integrity is the decision to stick to a certain ethical code, and act in ways that honor that code no matter what the circumstances (even- or indeed, especially, if no one is watching). These rules can be part of a religion, a philosophy, or a belief that you've come up with on your own terms, but establishing those rules is pretty much the most important thing you can do here.

Part of integrity is the ability to look back over the choices you've made in the past, and accept that not all of them have adhered to the moral code you would have liked. That's okay, too. Try not to waste time feeling guilty or embarrassed by them, but instead use them as jumping off points to establish what you would do now when faced with a situation such as the one you failed to handle correctly before.

Part of integrity is the trust and comfort in your own beliefs. You are secure in the things that you believe in, and therefore you don't need the validation of others to confirm that you are doing the right thing. Of course, taking on opinions and listening to other people's ideas are important, but the ability to make the difficult, but morally right, decision when no one else will is priceless.

The ability to believe in your own ethical code as correct (and, while there are no ways to measure what is a correct ethical code, take into account social customs and the law when constructing yours) means that your self-esteem is no longer tied to the praise or validation of other people. You are already confident that you are making the right choice.

You're also less likely to compromise on events and actions. Holding yourself and no one else accountable for the choices you make means that you can't transfer blame to someone else in your department, or your absent friend, or your spouse when things don't go to plan. If something fails to meet your moral code, you're far more likely to try and ensure that whatever choice you make is as close to your personal rules as possible.

You'll also be more empathetic to the problems others might have with you. While it can be difficult to take criticism, having someone call you out on your behavior, either past or present, or that time you acted outside your ethical code (perhaps without even realizing it) will allow you to both make amends with that person as well as watch out for dangerous behavior in the future.

Take into account their issues with your actions, and consider if this is a wider problem that may have affected other people. If they bring up past behavior, use it as an opportunity to tweak your code to make sure that nothing like this happens again. Your ethical code and value system are always works in progress, as you can't possibly have covered every moral dilemma you'll face during your lifetime, and adding to and taking away from it is fine, provided you stick to the rules that are there.

One of the most important ways that integrity will help you is by improving your relationships with those around you. Part of establishing yourself as a person with integrity is learning to respect other people's feelings towards you. This doesn't mean changing how you act every time someone has an issue with you, because they could find problems with the difficult decision you've made even if you're confident that it's the right one. But becoming more empathetic to how your actions can affect and hurt others will strengthen your friendships and romantic relationships.

Once you accept that building towards integrity is an ongoing task, you'll also learn how to evolve with new situations more quickly. Having an ethical code that broadly covers most situations will allow you to tackle a specific one with the mindset of "what would future me want current me to have done? What can I do to look back and be proud and certain in my decision?"

It's likely that you'll begin to feel more confident taking on new situations and challenges, and find yourself able to make more considered decisions as opposed to snap judgments that will come back to haunt you in the future. This is particularly important and useful on the professional playing field, and will allow you to gain the trust of co-workers who know you'll make the decision that is morally correct in your eyes.

Trust

Trust comes as a double-edged sword. You have to both put your trust in other people, and have other people put their trust in you.

The first of these—learning to put your trust in other people—can be a difficult one for some. It's often seen as weak or gullible, and many people have problems truly learning to be open and honest with any other person. There are many reasons for this, for example, if you've been lied to or cheated on in the past, you'll be more wary of jumping into another intimate, trusting relationship again.

It's important to get by these issues and put your trust in those who've earned it. It's not a matter of convincing yourself but rather allowing them to convince you. Don't be too eager to trust, and watch and listen to how that person acts around different friends and what topics they choose to bring up with you. If you feel like they have proved themselves trustworthy with your secrets, you'll find a whole new side of the friendship opening up.

It's much the same scenario with getting people to place their trust in you. There's no point playing at being a trustworthy person if you're simply not; pressuring or encouraging someone to place trust in you by sharing intimate details of their life seems like a quick way to jump into a trusting relationship, but you have to allow them to open up to you in their own time. Some people are extremely comfortable sharing things that others would deem for their own ears only; it all depends on who you're talking to. Prove yourself a trustworthy person, to yourself and others, before encouraging people to share personal details of their life with you.

Proving yourself a trustworthy person means more than just having people tell their secrets to you. What you do with the information that various people have given you is the important part. If they told you in strictest confidence, would you dream of telling anyone at all? Or would it find its way to your partner or spouse? Even if they told you something without adding the disclaimer that it had to be kept between the two of you, would you feel uncomfortable sharing that information with a mutual friend?

This is not a matter of sealing your lips about everything your significant other tells you, it's a matter of establishing ground rules of what you're allowed to do with this information. Simply qualifying it with the person who's telling you: "so, do you want to keep this between us?" or "I think Jenny might have something useful to say on the subject, do you mind if I talk to her about it?" will help define you as a person who can be trusted with information that is passed on to in confidence. Obviously you also have to stick to whatever you've agreed upon as well.

Being trustworthy can also be demonstrated in non-verbal ways. Trusting people to do things that they've said they'll do—and not constantly calling to check up on them or nudge them about the matter—will put it into people's heads that you yourself can be trusted with important things to do. Be sure to keep all your promises, and not to make them smaller than they are in your head, as what could be a five-minute favor to you could make all the difference for somebody else. Being reliable in your actions will give people more faith in your words too.

Being honest and open with friends—speaking from the heart, and giving truthful accounts of what has occurred and your reaction to it—will seriously help when it comes to building trust between you and the person you're building a relationship with. You'll learn that it's okay to be open and honest and trust someone with these opinions that you have, while the other person will surmise that you're an honest person who won't lie to them. It's a win-win.

Learning to trust and be trusted is a vital part of becoming a more open, happier person. While many of us feel the need to do everything ourselves for fear that someone else's involvement might mess it up in some way, learning to trust people with errands and favors will take some of that weight off your back.

Trust is a difficult thing to earn and, while you don't want to blindly every person who wanders into your life, making sure that you have a small group of people around you who you can genuinely trust helps immensely. Building that support system means you have people in place who you can trust if the worst happens (whatever it may be), and finding a group who you can trust with your most upsetting or troubling secrets can help you work through those issues with proper support.

When it comes to being trusted by other people, there is a completely different precedent. You are putting all of your trustworthiness on the table, and showing them that you deserve to be trusted. It can be intimidating and a little scary to have someone trust you completely, but it is a big help in terms of familial and personal relationships; if someone trusts you, they are less likely to go behind your back to cover things up and lie to you as they know that you can be told these problems or secrets, and keep them within an agreed group of people. People who trust you will have no real need to lie to you, and this in turn, will help you develop your trust in them.

Service to Others

Providing service to others demonstrates your compassion and your ability to put your own needs behind those of someone else's. It's probably the most tangible way to become a good person, as you'll be able to directly see the benefit of your help and work to other people.

A lot of people mistake doing something for someone else as weakness, as an indicator that this person has a complete inability to say no. This is simply not the case. While you want to pick and choose precisely who you are helping and why, choosing to help out another human being of your own free will is one of the most rewarding acts you can carry out.

You'll want to be careful where you give service and compassion, as not everyone will be as deserving of your help as others, but try not to become cynical. Remember that helping others out doesn't necessarily have to mean constructing a school with your bare hands and writing the textbooks yourself; it can be something as small as complimenting someone on their shoes when they walk by, or swapping out your functional shopping cart for the one that doesn't go straight that a family of four are trying to navigate round a supermarket.

Don't allow your service to become a way to compete with other people who are also doing good deeds. Focus on how it makes you feel and on the service you are providing for the person at hand; don't put down your efforts because the guy in the cubicle next to you at work is doing something on a bigger scale. Be proud of your achievements, and use that pride to fuel the urge to go and help someone else out. Helping out other people is really the culmination of the four areas we've covered before: accepting and taking on small tasks that will make someone's day better or easier as part of our moral responsibility.

There are many things that stop people getting involved with helping other people. A big part of that is embarrassment. How will they react? Will they think that I'm patronizing them? Will they get angry or aggressive? Sure, there's the possibility of that, but try to gauge the situation: Do they look as though they may become aggressive or attack you? Are they looking around to signal that they need help to other people? How would you feel if you were in the same situation and someone approached you? Basically, make sure that you're not going to be intimidating them or upsetting them in any way, and try not to find inner excuses to get out of helping someone when you know it's the right thing to do.

It can be nerve-wracking just approaching people on the street and offering them help. If you think this is too far out of your comfort zone, don't be afraid to sign up for charity work in the area. This could mean visiting a senior home for an afternoon to talk to the residents there. Or, it could be helping out at a school sport's day, or doing a few hours of work at a local charity. There are many organizations you can approach if you want to use your time in a way that helps others, and you'll likely feel more compelled to do it if you can see the palpable results of your efforts.

Providing services to others will help develop your compassion and your empathy, allowing you to more clearly understand the problems that those closer to home are feeling. It's also been proven that doing good deeds for other people will help boost your mood and help you relax (and you won't be torturing yourself all day with the image of that woman struggling up the stairs with a stroller and ten bags in tow, wondering if you should have intervened).

While you shouldn't treat these services as favors that should have to be repaid at some point, it's likely that your friends and family will find some way to show you that they appreciate your efforts. When you do good deeds you inspire people to act in a similar way and, if you're inspiring the people close to you, it's likely that you'll wind up benefiting in some way. It is important enough to stress again you should *not* be treating services as a swap, but rather a small act of kindness that you offer to someone else to increase your own ethical standing.

There's also the most obvious answer of all to this question of what being of service to others can do for you, which is that helping out other people will make you as a person feel good. There's an intense amount of satisfaction that comes from doing a good deed, and that happy, good-person glow doesn't diminish no matter how many times you help someone out. Helping people is something that many feel too nervous or unsure to jump into, so getting into the habit of helping people will get you noticed, whether it's personally or professionally. You'll find yourself falling into habits that will bring a smile to the faces of countless people you encounter, as well as bringing the biggest smile to your own face.

Arrogance: Its Characteristics and Destructive Impact

It's all well and good to know what characteristics good people have in common so you can emulate them. But what about the characteristics you need to avoid? Do you know what they are? In this book we would like to stay more focused on the positive. When you understand what it is that makes a person good, you will begin to pick up on what makes a person bad. It then becomes easier to avoid bad characteristics in favor of the good. However, it is still helpful to touch on a couple of the most destructive of bad traits: arrogance and greed.

If asked to describe characteristics of someone who is not good, or who could maybe even be described as bad, many people would say arrogance. There are other traits you could come up with like selfishness, pettiness, meanness, ignorance, and so on, but one of the most hated characteristics a person can have is arrogance. We don't like arrogant, conceited people.

And why is that? Take a minute to think about a person you don't like. This could be someone at work, or even an extended family member. What is it about the person that bothers you? Chances are that person is arrogant to at least some degree. It's an unsavory and distasteful characteristic, especially when not backed up by positive traits or success. This person probably puts other people down while elevating himself. He is mean to other people. He is ignorant because he already thinks he knows everything. He's probably also lazy because he thinks everything he does is great and can't be improved upon. All of this is connected to arrogance.

And this leads us to ask what exactly arrogance is and how it can be distinguished from confidence. Because we like confident people, right? Confidence doesn't make someone disliked, mean, or bad. Confidence is good, but it's a fine line that separates it from arrogance.

We are all at times guilty of being arrogant to some degree, but if you want to be a good person, you need to nip it in the bud. That starts with understanding what arrogance is. Arrogance is a person's belief that he or she is superior to other people. It is also the set of behaviors that follows from this belief and these are characterized by disparaging other people. In other words, if you are arrogant, you not only believe yourself to be better than others, but you treat the people around you badly as a result.

Arrogant people tend to belittle others. They behave as if they are invincible and as if the opinions, beliefs, and abilities of other people are inferior. They are often mean to other people, especially when in a position of power. They try to make other people feel like they have less worth.

Confidence, on the other hand, while also a belief in one's abilities, is based on fact and reality and does not take away from the abilities of others. Where arrogance is an inflated sense of ability and self-worth, confidence is mirrored by results and what people around you think of you. If you're confident, you believe that you can succeed at a particular task or at many things generally, but you don't necessarily think you are better than the people around you.

People who are confident do not belittle the people around them. They do not think they are perfect or invincible, nor do they believe themselves to be superior and worthy of having more things or more respect than other people. They are not unkind to other people and they respect the opinions of others. They know they have room for improvement and are willing to learn more.

These are the things that set arrogance apart from confidence. In reading these descriptions you can probably see how confidence is a positive trait and arrogance a negative trait; you see how good people may be confident, but they are never arrogant.

It's easy to grasp on the surface, but there is more to the idea of avoiding arrogance. There are real, concrete reasons that this is one of the worst of the bad traits you could have and that if you want to be a better person you need to work on your confidence while stamping out any tendencies to be arrogant:

Arrogance is mean.
By its very definition, arrogance is cruelty to other people. No matter how you measure goodness, being kind has to be a part of it. When you inflate your own sense of self-worth and your abilities, you put others down. An arrogant person actively believes he is better than others, and inevitably treats others badly. To avoid arrogance you have to know, truly know in your heart, that you are not better than other people. Even if you have certain skills that someone else lacks, even if you are kinder than the person in the next cubicle, and even if you are smarter than your sister, you are not better. If you think you are better, you will not be nice to the people you think are beneath you. An arrogant person in a position of power, like a boss at work, may even be mean to the point of being emotionally abusive.

Arrogance means you can't get better.

If you think you are truly great, then what's the point in learning more? What is the point in trying harder if you are already there? Arrogant people rarely improve because they believe they don't have to. If you accept humility and modesty, on the other hand, you will always be seeking to improve yourself, to learn new skills, to get better at work and relationships, and to be a better, kinder, and more worthwhile person. Arrogance is stagnation and laziness. Not seeking to improve yourself is a hindrance to both you and everyone else around you who could benefit from a better version of you.

Arrogance leads to failure.

This is closely related to the point above. A direct consequence of being so arrogant that you don't have room for improvement is failure. Not only will an arrogant person not seek to make improvements, he will also not ask for, nor take seriously, the opinions of others. Some things can be achieved alone, but our biggest successes as human beings come when we work together and collaborate. Collaboration means sharing ideas and strategies. If you can't take the ideas of other people and consider them valid, you are bound to fail at many of the things you do. This could be at work, but also in personal endeavors and in your relationships.

Arrogant people are lonely.

No one likes to be around someone who is arrogant. Of course, there are degrees of arrogance and some can be tolerated, but real arrogance is a threat to relationships. You can't develop a real and lasting bond with another person if you think you are better than that person. No one wants to be friends with someone who is arrogant and the arrogant person sees it as beneath him to be friends with many people. The end result is loneliness and detachment.

Arrogance is not the only bad trait of bad people, but it is one that leads to many others. It makes people mean, lazy, abusive, and horrible to be around. If you have any arrogance in you, it's time to stamp it out and relearn modesty and humility. It's not fun being wrong or not being good at something, but it is important to admit when you fall short. Open yourself up to the possibility that you are not the best at everything and that you have weaknesses. Ask for help and learn from the experiences of others. This will help you grow as a person and a direct consequence will be that you will be kinder and more relatable to others and you will be a better person.

<u>Greed: Seeking Fame and Fortune</u>

Another characteristic that many would cite as common among so-called bad people is greed. If there's anything we like less in another person than arrogance, it is greediness. It is an incredibly unattractive trait. Someone who is greedy sends out a strong message to others: I deserve more and better than you do.

What is greed? It's probably easier to understand than arrogance. Greed is the intense desire to have something, and usually something materialistic. Greedy people want money, fame, power, expensive things, or even food. They desire these things regardless of, and without thought to, the needs of others.

People who are greedy are easy to recognize. They want things and they want them badly. They will go to great lengths to get what they want. They will step on other people to get what they want. Greedy people are mean because they don't care about the needs of others. Greedy people are also selfish. They want to take, no matter what it does to other people.

A very relatable form of greed today is fame. In the age of internet videos and reality TV shows, being famous for a few minutes is more of a possibility than at any time in the past. If you want to get famous, you can probably do it. To do it, you have to have the intense desire, the greed, to go for it and not care if anyone gets hurt in the process, including yourself.

Think about most of the reality TV shows on today. Many of them are competitions. People are pitted against each other with a prize dangled in front of them like a carrot on a stick. These participants are greedy in two ways: they want that prize and will trample over the others to get it and they want to be famous. In fact, the greedier and more cutthroat the stars of these shows are, the more famous they become. It is a fact of our modern culture that greed and fame go hand-in-hand.

Another modern-day manifestation of greed can be seen in many big corporations and among their CEOs. Corporate practice in America today is dominated by greed. While many workers at the bottom make minimum wage, CEOs make millions. And what is the role of a CEO? At one time it was multi-faceted, but today the role of a CEO is largely to maximize profits for shareholders. It's all about wanting more, no matter the cost. Profits are expected to grow even if it means human rights violations in factories, child labor, and environmental disasters.

Greed has become a part of our everyday culture, and to many people it is considered good. It is a mark of success to be famous, to be cutthroat, to want more, to get better profits at the expense of individuals. This is a dangerous idea, and while no one would suggest you should let people walk all over you and take from you, greed is bad:

Greed actively hurts other people.

As with arrogance, the most important reason that greed and the pursuit of fame and fortune are bad is that they hurt other people. Sure, it's possible to get what you want without hurting others, but when you're greedy, that's not good enough. Greed is characterized by hurting or depriving others to get more of what you want. If you're greedy, you might spread a lie about a coworker to ensure you get the promotion instead of her. If you want to be famous on reality TV, greed will make you trick and scheme against others to win. If you want what someone else has, you might steal it.

Greed destroys relationships.

How can you ever have a good relationship if you're greedy? Relationships you have with people, from acquaintances to coworkers to friends, and lovers, all require give and take. You can't just take and expect to have a good, satisfying relationship. If you are a greedy person and have the good fortune to have relationships in spite of this negative trait, they won't last long unless you give to the other person as much as you take from them.

Fame will not make you special.

Being greedy for fame is likely a reaction to a desire to be special, to be one of the chosen few. Many people want to be famous today, but the truth is that fame does not make someone special. If you could meet a celebrity, you might be surprised to find that he or she has the same problems, worries, and issues that you have. Having such a strong desire for something that is ultimately meaningless is futile. Unless you genuinely want to use fame to do good things in the world, it isn't a worthy pursuit and it is simply a manifestation of greed.

Being greedy and materialistic is bad for your health.

Research has proven what wise people have always known, which is that greed is bad, not just for those around you, but also for you. If you are greedy about materialistic things, you are at a greater risk for developing depression, anxiety, and even physical ailments like headaches.

Overall, being materialistic keeps you from being happy. This is true for several reasons. The pursuit of things leaves you less time to spend on activities that will truly make you happy, like spending time with family or giving back to your community. Being materialistic also usually means that you have psychological issues that aren't being addressed. Trying to accumulate more things simply buries the issues further.

Being greedy makes it more difficult to recover from setbacks.

According to research conducted by psychologists, a greedy or materialistic disposition amplifies any kind of traumatic situation. The researchers showed that if two people experience the same kind of bad situation and one person is greedy and the other isn't, it is the person who is not greedy who will recover better and more quickly. The bad or traumatic event could be a car accident, a financial setback, or something much bigger, like a terrorist attack. A materialistic nature amplifies it and can lead to such mental health conditions as post-traumatic stress disorder.

Greed, fame, money, materialism: these are all manifestations of the same bad characteristic. Not only is greed bad for people in general, it's bad for the greedy person. The way to be a truly good person is to work toward being less greedy. We all pursue materialistic things to some extent, but as you try to become a better person, consider just how much you want those things, how greedy you are, and how you could learn to place less value on things you want.

Part of this will mean becoming more self-aware. Pay attention to how you interact with people. Do you put your own desires ahead of those of others regularly? Do you put too much focus on getting nicer things or succeeding at work? Do these pursuits get in the way of spending time with your family or friends? Do you have a lot of nice things, but no satisfying relationships? Consider your greed level and how much you value materialistic goods and you might be surprised at how much you could change for the better.

<u>Whose Happiness Matters Most?</u>

We have already talked about different ideas, philosophies, and systems for what it means to be good, or ethical. When you boil all of these down, you will realize that being good has a lot to do with happiness and well-being. Good equates with being happy. For there to be more goodness in the world, and for you to be someone who helps to make the world a better place, you need more people to be happier.

This leads to a couple of questions: What does it mean to increase happiness? And whose happiness is most important? To address the first is fairly simple. You are a human. You know what makes you happy. We're not talking about detailed, unique, or individualistic preferences and tastes. For example, just because eating macaroni and cheese makes you happy doesn't mean that putting more cheese and pasta into the world will increase happiness, although it might a little bit.

To determine what makes people truly happy, we need to be more philosophical. The first thing to consider is basic need. A person does not have a chance of being happy until her basic needs and rights are met. This means that people need to have shelter, enough to eat and drink, safety, meaningful work, and freedom from abuse and other types of mistreatment.

Beyond the basic needs, there are some universal truths about what makes us happy. In fact, researchers have answered this question for us pretty effectively by looking at happy people and what they have in common. Happy people are surrounded by family and friends. They are not materialistic and not concerned about keeping up with the materialistic goods that people around them have. They take pleasure in daily activities and they forgive others easily. They are grateful for what they have and the people in their lives.

What all this means for increasing goodness in the world and being a good person is that you need to consider these traits of happiness. Help people get their basic needs and rights met. Establish and maintain good relationships with other people. Get rid of greed and materialism. Be grateful for what you have and be grateful for the relationships you have. Find and engage in meaningful activities and help others do the same. Learn to forgive and apologize readily.

It all seems pretty simple in black and white print, but what about a balance between finding this happiness for you and helping others find it? Do you need to sacrifice your own happiness to help others? Is ensuring that you are happy enough to be a good person and to bring more goodness to the world? Or, can you do both?

This may seem contrary to the idea of this book, but you should focus on your own happiness first. If you have ever watched a talk show or makeover show in which a hardworking mom, who does everything for everyone and puts hers own needs last, gets a treat for a day or even a week, you have heard this idea before: you can't help others before you help yourself. That overworked mom feels guilty about a spa day or spending money on a new wardrobe, but the truth is that until she takes care of her needs she can't fully take care of the needs of her family.

There are other, more practical, physical, and immediate examples of this philosophy of putting oneself first. Anyone trained as a lifeguard will tell you that you have to make sure you are not going to drown before you can rescue someone. If you go under, you both go under. You can't save anyone if you get tired in the water, or hit your head and drown. On an airplane, the flight attendants always tell you that you have to adjust your own oxygen mask before helping anyone else with their fittings.

These ideas are more obvious, but the same rings true for the more general and abstract concept of being good and increasing happiness in the world. You can neglect yourself and go out into the world only spending your time and attention on others, but you won't be doing as much good as you could if you first made sure your own needs were met.

In order to do the most good in the world and to be the best person you can be to serve others, you need to be well and happy. Start by finding the goodness in yourself. Take care of your own needs. Find out what makes you happy, relaxed, and satisfied with life. Only then can you take what you know and spread it around to other people.

Of course, you should not get stuck in step one. Self-serving agendas are not good if it's all you focus on to the exclusion of other people. To be good you need to consider the wants, desires, and needs of others too. Once you have reached a point in your life at which you have your basic needs met, you are generally happy, and you feel like your life is good and you know what other people need, then you can start serving others.

As you begin to reach out to the world at large in your attempt to be a good person, consider that you still don't need to be truly selfless. There will still be times when you need to be self-serving. When you're exhausted from staying up late to help your teenage son work on a school project, go to bed. You will be no help to your other kids the next day if you don't get enough sleep. If you've been volunteering at a soup kitchen and you are emotionally burned out by what you experience there, take some time off. When you have recharged and refreshed you will be better able to put your best talents into service for others.

You should also be aware that your kind acts are generally those that help both you and others. There are almost no truly selfless acts. In most cases, a good deed is mutually beneficial. You are helping someone else, but you are also getting something out of it. This does not mean that you are doing a favor for someone with the expectation of getting something in return. That is the opposite of being altruistic and selfless. But without always realizing it, you get something good out of being good, as discussed earlier in this book.

You may also get involved in acts that are more obviously mutually beneficial, and there is nothing wrong with that as long as you are not demanding something that you shouldn't. For instance, there is nothing bad and everything good in exchanging help with a coworker. Maybe you can help him develop a slideshow for a presentation and teach him what you know about the software. In return he wants to help you craft that report because writing isn't your strength. By helping each other you are being good, not selfish. You are working together to help each other. Just because it is mutually beneficial doesn't mean that it isn't good or useful.

True selflessness means engaging in acts of kindness that you know can't be repaid. Taking a sick, stray dog to the vet and paying for his care is selfless. That dog can't repay you financially and he can't compensate you for the time you spent helping him. Serving a meal at a soup kitchen and giving up your Saturday afternoon to do so is selfless. The homeless eating there may be grateful for your actions, but they can't repay you.

Being selfless is an important part of being good, but don't make the mistake of assuming that it is everything. You can and should be concerned with your own happiness. You can and should also work with people who can also help you. Bringing goodness into the world means helping yourself, helping those who can help you back, and helping the truly helpless.

The Golden Rule

By now you must surely understand that the concept of being good is complicated. There are many ideas about how to be good and what it all means. A subject that at first seems so simple and intuitive becomes complicated and multi-faceted as you dig deeper. And yet, there is one simple principle that has stood the test of time when it comes to guiding right behavior.

For some people, being good can be reduced to a simple, yet famous statement, called the Golden Rule. Most often associated with Christianity, the idea behind the Golden Rule is common to almost all world religions and is very old. As it is most often worded, the Golden Rule says:

Do unto others as you would have them do unto you.

In other words, treat people the way you would want them to treat you. In many situations you can apply this one line to help you decide what action is best. It is a very simple way to think about being good, and of course, it has imperfections. As a general rule, you can't possibly make being good any simpler. Time has been good to the Golden Rule, and it still often applies today. An addition to this statement is often called the Silver Rule:

Don't do anything to others that you would not have them do to you.

It is the reverse of the Golden Rule, but equally important. You want someone to be kind to you when you're in a bad mood, so you do the same for your spouse when he's feeling crabby. On the other hand, you also wouldn't want him to be nasty to you just because he had a bad day at work. You, then, should strive not to be mean to him when you have a bad day at work. The Golden and Silver Rules both work in many situations.

Christianity co-opted the Golden Rule and named it as such, but a more generalized, global version of this rule is called the ethic of reciprocity. It means exactly the same thing and the idea has been around in a number of cultures for thousands of years with different kinds of wording and applications.

So, is the Golden Rule all you really need to guide you to be a good person? If only it were so simple. It's a good start and it works often. Try it the next time you're in doubt about what to do. For instance, you saw a coworker steal someone else's lunch from the office refrigerator. You know the wronged party would like to know who did it, but you feel bad outing the thief. Put yourself in the position of each of these people and ask what you would want them to do. It can help clear up a lot of situations. Maybe if you were the thief you would hope that the person who caught you would tell you in private and give you the chance to come clean.

Applying the Golden Rule, even if it doesn't clarify an answer to an ethical dilemma for you, can be helpful in guiding you to be more empathetic. It forces you to put yourself in someone else's shoes. We too often ignore what other people are thinking and feeling. When you actively try to imagine what other people are going through, you become more empathetic and kinder.

You can also use the Golden Rule as a general guideline for how to be. What kind of person do you like to be around? Be that person. The Golden Rule is all about empathy. It means spending time thinking about what other people are thinking and feeling, what they want, and what will make them happy. The more time you spend in consideration of the feelings of others, the better a person you will become. There are a number of ways in which the Golden Rule can guide your general behaviors:

Be empathetic always. Consider the feelings of others instead of only thinking about your own.

Be friendly. Do you prefer friendly or terse people? Be the friendly and helpful person that others like to be around.

Be kind. This seems obvious, but we are all guilty of forgetting how important simple kindness is. Think about times when someone was kind to you. Maybe a sales clerk smiled at you and complimented your hair. A driver may have let you in as you waited to make a turn. Or that person you spilled your drink on at the movies didn't get mad at you. These little acts of kindness make a difference.

Avoid prejudice. Do you like it when people prejudge you? Probably not, so why do it to others. Be more understanding and make a point to get to know people before passing judgement.

Don't retaliate. If someone treats you badly or is unkind, don't reciprocate. Following the Golden Rule has nothing to do with how anyone else actually behaves. Do what is right according to you, not according to how you have been treated.

Help those who are down. We have all been down at some point in our lives, and what did we want then? A helping hand would have been a lifesaver. Be that helping hand for people who are down, from someone who dropped her groceries in the parking lot, to your neighbor who lost his job and needs help with child care, and everyone in between.

Listen to others. We all want to be heard. Don't forget that just because you want to be heard that others don't also need to be heard. Learn to listen.

Following the Golden and Silver Rules is not a bad idea, but there are flaws in thinking that this is all you need. Throughout history the ethic of reciprocity has largely been used within cultural groups. Outsiders are not always considered to be worthy of the same consideration.

Another issue with the Golden Rule is that it is an ideal. Idealized philosophies are not always easy to live up to and failure can be disheartening. Realize that you will not be able to make every decision fall into line with the ethic of reciprocity. Some situations will just not allow you to do exactly what you would wish someone would do for you. Perhaps an addition to the Golden Rule would be to say that you should do unto others to the best of your ability.

There is also the difference in values to consider. What one person values, another may not, which means that what you want may not at all be what someone else wants. And then there are some situations in which the Golden Rule simply falls flat. Should a murderer not be sentenced to prison because a jury wouldn't want to be sent to prison? Of course the rule is going to fail in a situation like this. It isn't a perfect prescription for living a good life.

There are a few reasons not to rely solely on the Golden Rule to guide your goodness, but it is a fine place to start and a principle to which you can return often. Just use your good sense when you refer back to it to decide what to do in a given situation. The most important thing to do is to be as empathetic as the Rule suggests you should be. Always consider what other people need, want, and feel, to guide you to do good things.

Common Ethical Dilemmas

We have all faced ethical dilemmas. Sometimes they come up at work. Other times they arise in our personal relationships. When you're trying to be good and do good things, you will find that you come up against some gray areas from time to time. That's why they are called dilemmas. As we already have seen, deciding on the best thing to do in any given situation is not as straightforward as it may seem at first. The Golden Rule doesn't always work and is too simple for many situations.

Before you tackle all of the ethical situations that arise in your life, you will hopefully have given careful consideration to what your ethical system is. You have thought about what you value and whether or not there are any moral guidelines you want to follow. With a basic understanding of your own ethical code, you will be better able to handle ethical dilemmas.

For instance, imagine you are at work and you decide to spend ten to fifteen minutes getting some personal things done. You need to set up a doctor's appointment, call your child's teacher, and do a few other small things. You want to get it done at work because you know you will be swamped by other things once you get home and your office is quiet right now.

If part of your ethical code is that you should never use company time for personal business, this would be an unethical situation. On the other hand, if you value doing your job well and getting your work done, regardless of whether that happens in the office or after hours, you could consider the situation acceptable. You have to decide which is ethical, unless of course your workplace has a strict policy about personal business in the office. In that case it isn't up to your discretion.

Don't feel as if you have to have your ethical code completely and accurately mapped out right now, but you should give it some thought. You should also consider it a flexible code. As different situations and dilemmas arise, you can consider changing what you think is right or wrong. It also helps to consider some common ethical dilemmas in the abstract so that it is easier to face them in reality:

Harassment or abuse at work
The workplace is fraught with ethical dilemmas and they are particularly hard to come to a decision on because you need your job and your income. It's not easy to risk the boss's favor or to risk losing your job just to do the right thing. For example, if you see someone at work being verbally abused or sexually harassed by

the boss, what can you do? You could confront the harasser, talk to the human resources department, or pretend you didn't see it.

Mistreatment of customers

What if you realize that your company or someone you work with is deceiving customers, lying about a product, inflating prices, or otherwise mistreating customers? Speaking up about it may mean risking your position.

Taking advantage of position

If you are in a management position have you ever had the opportunity to get away with something that workers lower down the totem pole would not? The guidelines for behavior at work are meant for everyone, but as a manager you know you can get away with more. Should you?

Falling into the "everyone else is doing it" trap

This can happen anywhere, but is common in the workplace. You know you aren't supposed to take breaks except at your scheduled break times, but other employees do it all the time. They step outside for a smoke or to check their phones whenever the feel like it. If others can do it, should you?

To be a whistle-blower or not to be a whistle-blower

Laws and policy changes have made it easier and safer for whistle-blowers to come forward and point out unethical practices at work. However, every workplace is different and by coming forward you always take a risk. You have to decide if it is worth doing what is right.

You know that your friend's teen is getting into the wrong crowd

Work is not the only place for ethical dilemmas. In your personal relationships you face them all the time. This one could take many different forms. Should you speak up about what you see going on with your friend's or your sister's kids? Or should you mind your own business?

You see a friend/family member making relationship mistakes, again

It's hard to stand by and watch someone you care about make the same mistakes over and over again. Is it your place to give advice? Will that person consider your advice or are you just straining your relationship with him or her and butting in where your opinion isn't wanted?

Your good friend makes an offensive joke

You don't think it's funny and you are offended by it, but you're not sure if you should say something about it or just let it go for the sake of your friendship.

You find out that someone is having an affair

This is a pretty common one and the solution is perplexing. Your best friend's husband is cheating. Do you tell her or do you leave it alone? Do you confront the husband or the woman with whom he is having an affair? It's a thorny situation.

Cheating in school

Cheating in school, for youngsters and adult students, is a tough dilemma. Do you cheat just a little to get the grade you need or are you strict about cheating and never engage in it? What do you do if you see someone else cheating on a test or a paper?

You want to save money at the movies, so you lie about your age

You can justify this move by assuming the movie theater is a big corporation and that they charge too much anyway, or that they never check for age, or by saying that everyone does it. Does that make it OK?

You eat free samples at the grocery store with no intention to buy anything

So this one seems pretty benign in comparison to others, but it is worth consideration. Does the store put out samples knowing that some people will try them without buying? Or do they lose money on samples in the hopes that they will help with sales?

You could probably think up a hundred more ethical dilemmas, and you should. Considering ethical situations before and as they happen can help you decide how to do what is right. A good exercise for being more ethical is to journal on these situations as they come up in your daily life. Make note of what happened, what the dilemma was, what you decided to do, why, and what the result was. Reflection helps us to make better decisions and will help you clarify what your ethical standards are.

<u>Putting Relationships First</u>

Another way to approach becoming the new, more ethical you, is to reflect on where relationships stand in your life. As we mentioned earlier, the happiest people, according to research, value spending time with family and friends. Being surrounded by the people they care about and love is one of the things that makes them happiest. Happiness is goodness, and therefore relationships play a big role in being good.

Think about your values. What do you place the most value on in your life? What do you need more than anything, beyond your basic needs and rights? Is it work? Is it material things? Is it time alone? Or is it your relationships? Most people would answer with the latter. We are social animals and without other people we are nothing.

There is another way to consider this: If goodness means being good to oneself and being good to other people, then relationships must come out on top above things like work and material goods. If you want to be a truly good person you need to start putting relationships out in front, in all situations. Once you have taken care of yourself, being good means helping other people, and when you lead with relationships you do it automatically.

Love is all there is (and all you need?)
It's a cliché and a famous song lyric, but it turns out that love really is at the pinnacle of our lives. It may not really be all there is or truly all you need, but it is the most important thing in our lives and it underlies all our relationships. A 75-year study from Harvard University investigated what makes a good, satisfying, and happy life, and found that love was the answer.

The study followed participants from childhood to old age to see what people value, how values change over time, and what makes people happy and fulfilled. The top finding was that love was the most important factor for a happy and good life for the participants. The researchers also found that the relationships we have are really the only things that ultimately matter in life. People in the study who were successful, wealthy, and healthy, but had no loving relationships were not happy.

The study also pointed out how crucial it is to connect with people. The more ways in which the participants made connections throughout their lives the happier they were. Connections that were deep and loving, and even just friendly or work-related, were all important to life satisfaction for the study participants. Those connections became more and more important with age.

Putting relationships first will make you a happier person, but will also help you spread the happiness to others. By focusing on relationships you de-emphasize the things in life that matter less: money, career, success, material things. You also make people feel good and inspire them to do the same. Make relationships the focus of all areas of your life to be a better person.

Personal relationships

These are the most important relationships we ever have. Our connections to our family, our friends, and our significant others are the most important and impactful relationships in our lives. They affect us more than anything else in life and they deserve attention, time, and devotion.

This might seem obvious, but the truth is that too many people take their closest relationships for granted. We never fully appreciate our loved ones until it's too late. But if you can come to this realization now, you can turn it around. It's easy to justify not spending enough time with your loved ones. There always seems to be something else to do. You spend too much time at work. You spend too much time looking down at your smartphone. You prioritize your workout over time with family. You might even spend too much time doing volunteer work in an attempt to be a good person when you should be devoting more time to your personal relationships.

Realizing that your personal relationships and the people you love are more important than anything else in life means making changes. Leave work at a decent hour whenever you can. Have dinner with your family and outlaw phones at the table. Get your loved ones involved in the charity work you do or your exercise regime. Whatever it is that prevents you from valuing your relationships, make a change and prioritize people over things and activities.

Family may be most important, but don't let your friendships suffer at their expense. Friends are important too. Spend more time with friends in the real world, talking, and less time on social media or at work.

Work relationships

This emphasis on the importance of people and relationships should bleed over into other areas of your life. Your family and friends may be most important, but your work relationships take up a lot of your time every day. They're important too. You may even develop some very meaningful friendships with coworkers if you take the time to get to know the people around you every day.

Your work relationships don't have to become friendships, but when you put relationships first in every context you will see some positive results. What does this look like at work? Think about what you currently value in the workplace? What gets most of your attention? Probably getting your work done, right? What if you put people ahead of that? What would happen?

Maybe you would find that you could help someone who is struggling with a task and still get your own work done. You'll feel better when you promote a coworker who did a good job on something instead of blowing your own horn. You will become a better member of a team and your work will probably benefit. You might even get more notice from the boss and advance at work because you started focusing more on the people around you and your relationships to them, and less on getting ahead or earning a bonus.

Acquaintance relationships

Most of your relationships take place in your personal life and your work life. But what about all those other people you encounter every day? You interact and talk with many people, like your mail carrier, or the bartender at your favorite restaurant. What about that fellow runner you say hi to each morning as you pass each other or the clerk that sells you gas or your morning paper?

These people are acquaintances, and while they may not be your family, friends, or coworkers, you do have relationships with them. Don't leave them out of your plan to become a better person and to put relationships first. When you step up to the counter to get what you need at the drugstore, you may be in a sour mood, but think about how the woman behind the counter is feeling. She's probably tired of standing and maybe other customers have been rude to her. How can you make her day better? Smile and as her how she's doing. It's that simple to put effort into acquaintance relationships and to make others feel good.

Relationships rule the world and our lives. It's all too easy to get caught up in believing that other things are more important. It's easy to get lazy about relationships. When you start living by the belief that people and relationships are more important than anything else, you will become a better person and you will inspire other people to be better.

<u>Increasing Good in the World</u>

Now that you have decided to be a good person and to really put the work into figuring out what that means and what you need to do, it's time to take your mission beyond your own front door. Part of increasing the good in the world is related to you deciding to be better and putting it into action. As you take actions to be a better person, you are already raising the level of goodness in the world.

If you're reading this book, though, you are probably not going to be satisfied with being a passive do-gooder. You want to make a bigger impact and you want your efforts to really make a difference. You care about people and you want your life to matter and to have impacted the world in a positive way. That means you need to focus on not just being a good person, generally, but also on making a bigger difference. You need to focus your efforts to consciously help people and increase the good in the world. In addition to taking care of yourself and making sure you are a good person, there are three main ways in which you can make the world a better place.

Focusing on people and relationships

People are at the heart of goodness. The main reason to be good and to do good deeds is to make people happier and to ensure that people have their needs met. With that in mind, the most obvious way to do good in the world is to help other people. Make decisions and take actions with the needs and well-being of people in mind and you will begin to make the world better.

It's all about taking your focus away from things that are less important than people and living by that guiding rule. When you make choices on a daily basis, make people the center of your internal debate, not things. For example, your neighbor just had hip surgery, and while she is recovering well, she is having a hard time moving around. Should you spend a couple extra hours a week helping her get some yard work done? Or should you use that time to earn more overtime at work so you can buy that new TV you've been wanting? Put people before things and you make the world a better place.

As we have said before, this shouldn't come at the expense of your own needs and happiness. Take care of yourself, but also take care of other people. You don't have to make huge sacrifices to help others most of the time. Just doing small favors for people, or being kind always, no matter what your current mood, you are helping people.

The simple act of smiling at other people can even make a big difference. Smiling sends a powerful message to others and can brighten moods and lift someone out of a funk from a bad day. Smiling can even induce people to do better things, according to research, which means that by smiling more you can amplify the good you see in the world. Smiling, as the study found, improves peoples' moods and their inclination to do good deeds. Smiling is contagious, so keep doing it, even when you don't feel like it. It is the easiest way you can increase the good in the world.

Volunteer work

Another way to make the world a better place is to volunteer your time to good works. It requires more conscious effort than just being good and putting people first. You have to sacrifice your time, and sometimes your money, to volunteer for good causes, but it is worth it. This is where you really get to see the impact that your good intentions make.

You also have a lot of options when it comes to volunteering. We have talked a lot about people and how people are at the heart of being good. Consider helping with charity groups that help people. You can volunteer at a homeless shelter, with an organization that helps the developmentally disabled, or to tutor disadvantaged children.

People are your main focus, but that doesn't mean you can't volunteer to help with other causes that are important to you. The world itself is a big place that needs protection. If you love animals, work with an animal welfare or conservation group. If you are passionate about the environment, find a group that cleans up pollution or educates the public about climate change.

The most important thing is to pick a line of work about which you are passionate. The more engaged you are with the volunteer work, the more good you will do. Don't let anyone discourage you from your choice, even if they try to tell you that there are worthier causes. If animals are your passion and you want to help at a local shelter, don't listen to someone who tells you that working with children is more important. All causes that increase the good in the world are worthy of your time and commitment.

Another consideration to make when you decide how and where to volunteer is your own talent. Do you have a particular skill that can make a difference to a cause? If you are a writer, you can write grant proposals for various non-profit groups and help them raise funds. If you're a teacher, you can help underserved teens by working with them at school. Consider your own talents, how you can best contribute, and where your passion is when deciding how to volunteer and you will do the most good.

Paying it forward

Finally, as you decide how you can increase the good in the world, it is important to consider the pay it forward philosophy. Most people know this phrase from the movie of the same name, but it is a valid, life-guiding philosophy with a non-profit organization to back it up. It's a simple, but effective idea: to make the world a better place, and to increase the goodness in the world, be kind to people, particularly strangers. It's similar to the idea of random acts of kindness. When you are kind to people, even those you don't know, without ulterior motives or expectation of getting anything in return, you make the world better and more caring.

The idea is simple: If you are kind to strangers, they will be kind to the strangers they encounter. They will pay it forward. As a rule, you should consciously pay kindness forward, but by doing so you will also encourage people on a subconscious level. It's like the research on smiling. If a simple smile can induce people to engage in more courteous behaviors, think what a good deed can do. Here are some examples of what you can do randomly for strangers to pay it forward and inspire others to do the same:

Help out that person in line for coffee who is a dollar short.

Help the older woman struggling to lift her groceries into her car.

Speak up when someone is being bullied.

Pick up that wallet and chase after the person who dropped it in the parking lot.

Hold the door or the elevator for the person behind you.

Give your hardworking waiter a big tip.

Help someone up who slips on an icy sidewalk.

Give an encouraging smile to someone who looks sad.

There are so many ways in which you can make the world a better place. It's about much more than simply being a good person. You have to act on that idea of goodness. Focus on people, be kind to strangers, and take time to give back and you will be actively increasing the good in the world.

<u>Modeling Virtuous People</u>

Having a role model or two is a great way to find inspiration and motivation no matter what your goals are. When you have people to look up to and to inspire you, you have a direct model for what you consider to be good behavior and right actions. Having someone to model your choices on is not necessary. You can develop your system of ethics on your own and decide how best to be a good person without inspiration from others. However, finding role models in the world can be a powerful way to make the job of being good easier.

Start by looking around you. Ask yourself if you know anyone whom you admire for their virtues, how they treat others, and how they treat themselves, and how they spend their time and energy. The best role model is someone you know and can interact with. Maybe you have always admired your father for the way he acts, how he gives back, and for the way he interacts with other people. He can be your role model.

You might also want to consider having a mentor. This is a more formal way to emulate a role model. A mentor is someone who actively guides you, and while it is a relationship that you usually develop for your career, mentorship can be about anything you want it to be. Don't be afraid to ask someone you admire to be a mentor. If this is a truly good person, he or she will either accept or let you down kindly and give you a good reason for doing so. If you do have a mentor, spend time together, discuss goals, and learn from his or her experiences so that you can make better choices in your life.

Being able to emulate people whom you actually know and can spend time with is the most powerful form of role modeling. However, it also helps to have even loftier inspirations. Famous and historical figures that are traditionally considered virtuous and good have had a major impact on the world. Admiring and emulating these people is a great way to find inspiration in your own life for being a better person. Here are just a few to get you started. These people had many virtues, but most are known for one or two in particular. Read up on these figures and be inspired if you are struggling to be kind, loving, selfless, or brave.

The Dalai Lama – Wisdom and Kindness

His Holiness the 14th Dalai Lama of Tibet is the leader of Tibetan Buddhism and an important world figure today. He exemplifies many virtues with his words and actions, but is particularly known for being wise and kind. He believes that the most important actions in life are being compassionate and kind to other people. He also works tirelessly around the world to help people from different religions and cultures come together to better understand each other and to bring more peace to the world. He inspires people every day and can do the same for you if you follow his teachings of compassion and understanding.

Mother Teresa - Selflessness

No one embodies the virtue of selflessness better than Mother Teresa of Calcutta. A nun and missionary, she spent most of her life living in India caring for the poor and sick, the people no one else would touch. She was awarded the Nobel Peace Prize and is on the path to canonization as a saint in the Catholic Church. She lived a life of charity and gave nearly all she had for other people. Thousands of people were cared for by her and millions more reap the benefits of those who have emulated her. Let Mother Teresa's selflessness inspire you to give of yourself to those who have less.

Martin Luther King Jr. and Mahatma Gandhi – Courage

Both of these civil rights leaders knew that peaceful protest was the best way to effect change. King was inspired by Gandhi who led peaceful marches and protests in India, directly leading to emancipation from Great Britain. Both leaders faced daunting odds and violent threats and yet persevered to make real changes happen. It takes courage to lead people against injustice and against violence without using violence. When you are feeling less than brave in the face of doing what you know is right, let the actions of these two inspire you.

Abraham Lincoln – Leadership and Hard Work

Considered by many to be our greatest president, Lincoln's greatest achievement may have been the emancipation of slaves, but he was also a just and good leader in many other ways. He exemplified what it means to be a leader that people want to follow. He cared about his important job and served the people of the U.S. in the ways that he thought were the best. He is also known for being a hard worker. He started out life on a farm and worked to become a lawyer, a politician, and finally the president. He changed the course of U.S. history, and Lincoln can also be a guide for how to lead and an inspiration for hard work.

The Buddha – Self-Improvement

As you now know, being a good person begins with you. You have to work on yourself before you can change the world or help others. No figure from history better exemplifies this idea than the Buddha. Now often worshipped in a God-like way, the Buddha was a real man and his teachings led to the formation of the religion of Buddhism. He was born a prince, but took on an ascetic way of life and spent years meditating to find wisdom. He achieved a state of enlightenment and spread his message to his followers, teaching others how to do the same. The Buddha is the perfect example of someone who understood that self-awareness and self-improvement has to come before helping others.

Jesus - Love

Love is all there is, according to Jesus, who is possibly the most famous of all historic figures. Whether you believe he was the son of God and the Messiah, or not, what is clear is that Jesus loved his fellow men and women and he taught his followers to do the same. He taught people to love their neighbors and to turn the other cheek. Not only did Jesus preach love, he acted on it. He didn't just help marginalized and needy people, he truly loved and cared for them. Jesus exemplifies love and that is what everything boils down to in the end. If you love yourself and other people, you will do good deeds in the world.

Authentic Self: Maneuvering in the Virtual World

By now, if you have done the work, you are more self-aware, you are working on making yourself a better person, you are working on your own needs and happiness, and you are developing a personal code of ethics while also taking inspiration from those people who have gone before you on a quest to make the world a better place.

You know who you are and what you value and you have made a commitment to being true to this new, authentic self. You want to be you and you want to be a good person, no matter what the situation. This means sticking to your values and ethics even while in the virtual world, and that is not always an easy task.

Perhaps the main reason that ethics and normal ways of behaving fly out the window when people get online is because we are not coming face-to-face with each other. When we can't see or hear another person, it's easier to be less kind. What makes online situations even worse is anonymity. When someone hides behind a fake or anonymous profile, he can be nasty and not feel too bad about it because no one knows who he is.

People say and do things online that they would never say or do to a person in the real world. Bullies thrive in the online world and we even have a special name for them: trolls. They live to ridicule people and start fights for no real reason other than because they get a kick out of it. It can be tough not to fight back against these bullies, and from time to time, it's even tempting to be unkind when you know you won't be called out for it outside the virtual world.

The internet is a haven for trolls saying mean things to people in the comments sections of blogs, on photos, and on social media posts. The anonymity of the internet provides an environment in which people feel less inhibited and freer to say things that hurt other people. You may not be the bully at heart, but when people start slinging mud, it's tempting to join in. It may even feel like you are doing good by telling the trolls what you think of them. But by stooping to their level, you only make the situation worse.

How do you maintain your authentic self and continue to be the good person you want to be in an atmosphere of trolling, bullying, and anonymous hate? The best way to stay true to yourself would be to stay out of situations in which you might be tempted to stray from your chosen values and ethics. This would mean not reading comments sections and not using social media sites at all and that is not necessarily practical or possible.

With a new focus on people and relationships, it's not a bad idea to remove you from the online world when possible and to spend more time with people in the real world. We tend to lose the connections we have with people when we spend too much time online or texting on our phones. When you can, hang out with people face-to-face, and spend less time on social media or other virtual locations. This way you concentrate on the relationships that are important to you and avoid much of the negativity online.

Being the bully is not the only way that being online can distract you from the good person you want to be. Ignoring what you see happening online is also at odds with your new, better self. As the saying goes, "If you are not a part of the solution, you are a part of the problem." Standing by and doing nothing, in reality and in the virtual world is as bad as doing something mean.

To continue to be true to you even when navigating the virtual world you need to make a commitment to stand up for people who get bullied. If you see someone making nasty comments to someone, speak up, but don't engage the bully in a taunting match. Tell that troll that you think they should be kinder and let it go at that. Just that one statement will make a world of difference to the person being bullied.

You can also take this a step further and reach out to anyone you see getting bullied or harassed online. Contact that person and tell them that you don't agree with the things the trolls say and that you are available to talk if they need someone to open up to. Putting yourself out there to help another person online is a brave and important thing to do. We have all heard the stories of people getting bullied online who go on to commit suicide. By reaching out you could make someone's day or you could save someone's life.

Sticking with your code of ethics, your values, and your authentic self is important no matter where you are. When you're in the grocery store, at home with family, riding the bus, in the office, or online, you need to be the new you always. Be good and do good things wherever you are to do the most good in the world. Don't let this part of you slide online. Avoid the nastiness if you can by staying out of those places where trolls most like to stir things up, but when you can't help but be online, stay true to you.

<u>Dealing with a Bad World</u>

The online, virtual world may seem like a simple place to navigate compared to the real world some days, especially if you watch the news regularly. It seems like bad news is the only news we get and it's not just natural disasters, it's also people being horrible to other people, to animals and to the environment. What is more disheartening is that a lot of bad news comes from our leaders and large corporations. What are we supposed to do when those who should be guiding us and those who seem too big to fight against are not being good?

It's easy to go with the flow, to follow, and to do what everyone else is doing, or at least what we perceive everyone else to be doing. Studies have proven this to be true. As just one example, consider littering. We all know intellectually that we shouldn't throw garbage on the ground or in the water, and yet most of us do it sometimes. Research has shown that we do it because we see everyone else doing it. We imitate the actions of others.

If you are in an area with litter all around, you probably won't think twice about dropping your paper cup on the ground and walking on. On the other hand, if you are somewhere that is clean and litter-free, you will think that littering isn't done here and so you won't do it. We follow the crowd. We follow what seems normal and what seems expected, most often without even thinking about it.

This can be a good thing, and evolutionarily speaking it has probably kept us alive as a species. We are social creatures and we learn behaviors from each other. Many of those are positive behaviors, but this tendency can be bad too.

Littering is just one example, but it illustrates the larger problem: if all we see in the world seems to be people doing bad things, it's hard to do the right thing. Doing bad things seems like the norm and it becomes even more of a struggle to stand up for what is right and to do things differently.

When you watch or read the news, you see all the bad things going on in the world. You read about how badly people behave and treat other people. It starts to seem normal. This doesn't mean that we should ignore the news and not know what's going on in the world, but it does mean that we need to be more conscious of how the bad in the world affects us. When you are more aware of what impacts your behaviors and choices, you have the power to change it.

Bad news also gives us a sense of hopelessness, according to research. We hear bad news constantly and it makes us feel as if the world is in such a bad state that nothing we can do will make any difference. No donation of time or money will help change things when the situation is so bad. The same research tells us that being bombarded with bad news about the world slowly chips away at an optimistic attitude, which isn't surprising.

The bad news we hear also lead us to overestimate just how bad things are. For example, parents feel more protective of their kids than they did a few decades ago. They think that kidnapping and abductions are a bigger problem today than ever before, even though there is no solid evidence to back up that idea. When we hear bad news, we make big assumptions, lose our optimism, and lose the will to try to do good and the hope that things will get better. It's your job as someone striving to be good to fight this sense of hopelessness.

And there is hope for doing good in a bad world. In the studies related to littering, what researchers found was that establishing a positive norm changed behaviors. In one study the researchers put flyers on car windshields in several parking lots. In those in which there was already a significant amount of litter on the ground, most people removed the flyer and threw it on the ground. In cleaner parking lots, most people found a garbage can or put the flyer in their cars.

By presenting positive situations and making people perceive positive behaviors and choices as the normal way of things, their behaviors and choices can be altered for the better. It would be great if the news media would take that message to heart and include more stories of people doing good things, but it's not likely to happen.

This means it is up to you to be someone who sets the standard for good behavior. How can you be good in a bad world? You do it by setting an example for other people. This might be the most powerful lesson you learn about being good. Being good isn't just for you. It isn't just your actions. It affects everyone around you. The more people make good choices and do good deeds, the more normal it will seem and the more other people will follow suit. Badness creates more badness, and goodness creates more goodness. It is a simple, but powerful concept and one that can motivate you as you struggle to make the right choices when it seems like badness is all around you.

This concept also suggests another solution. When the bad in the world is getting you down and sucking your will to do good things, all you need to do is remove yourself from the bad news and the bad people and surround yourself with goodness. On those particularly challenging days, when it seems like there is no point, turn off the news, go offline, and meet up with friends or family. Go to your favorite place to volunteer and put in some time. Spend time with your pets or go to the park and enjoy some quiet time in nature. Surround yourself with goodness in a bad world and you will be inspired and motivated to keep up the good fight.

Conclusion

Deciding to be a good person, or a better person, is a simple choice. However, once you get into the details of what it means to be good and how to implement a plan to increase the goodness in the world, it starts to get more complicated. Start by assessing what you want to get out of this project and transformation. Remember that being good is good for you and for others. You will get something out of this process beyond simply helping others.

Being good means putting effort into first deciding what it means to be good. You have to take time and effort to decide what being good means to you. You need to reflect on what you value the most and what your personal ethical code will be. Think about your religious and spiritual beliefs and decide if any moral codes will come into play in your mission to bring goodness to the world.

Investigate the characteristics of people who are good. What traits are most important to you? Understand what it means to have honor and integrity and to be trustworthy and humble. Consider service to others and how that increases the good in the world. Come up with other traits you want to emulate. Also think about the traits that are not very good. Reflect on arrogance and greed and decide if you indulge in them too often. Make a conscious choice to avoid these characteristics and to be more aware of your behaviors and actions so you can check yourself when you slip up and make a decision that you aren't proud of.

Realize that you have to consider your own happiness while you also want to make life better for other people. Your own needs, rights, and certain desires should be met before you can help others. Caring for oneself is a part of being good. It may be selfish, but it isn't bad. When you increase goodness by making life better for people, include yourself among people. You have to be happy, satisfied, and fulfilled in order to do the most good.

Once you have worked on yourself, remember that to help people you need to be people-centric. Put people and relationships ahead of everything else. In the end, people and relationships are what really matter, not material goods, success at work, or anything else. Think about the Golden Rule and how, simple though it is, it can apply to many situations and help guide you as you try to put people at the center of all choices you make.

For those situations that are too complicated to rely on that timeless principle, research can help. Read up on and learn about common ethical dilemmas and think about how you would proceed. When you prepare for tricky situations you will be better able to make a choice that you feel is right when it actually happens to you. It also helps to find role models, both in your life and from history, to help guide you when you aren't sure what to do or if you fear you might not be brave enough to do the right thing. Mentors and role models can help inspire and motivate you to be better.

Once you have done all of your homework and you have reflected and thought about what it means to be good, it's time to start thinking about the concrete things you can do to increase goodness in the world. Decide what kinds of philanthropic acts you can get involved in, the volunteer work you can do, and how to pay it forward with strangers and friends alike. And, finally remember to keep to your authentic, good self as you navigate the virtual world.

If you can take all these steps and really put in the time and the effort to try to be a good person, you will reap the rewards. You will be happier, healthier, and will live a more satisfying and rewarding life. Best of all, you will be actively making the world better and improving the lives of others.

JR00037

Printed in Great Britain
by Amazon